Thomas Balinger

Merlin Songbook

for beginners

Christmas Carols

for Merlin (M4) in D tuning (D-A-D)

Other titles by Thomas Balinger:

The Dulcimer Songbook
The Ukulele Songbook – 50 All Time Classics
The Baritone Ukulele Songbook
American Harmonica Songbook

Thomas Balinger
Merlin Songbook for beginners, Christmas Carols for Merlin (M4) in D tuning (D-A-D)

© 2018

Revised Edition 2019

ISBN: 9781731317278

Preface

Hello fellow players,

and welcome to my collection of Christmas tunes for the Merlin (M4).

All songs have been arranged for easy **Merlin in D tuning (D-A-D)** for the beginning player. Chord symbols, chord diagrams and melody tab have been added to the standard notation to make playing these songs as easy and straightforward as possible.

At the end of the book there's a short section on tuning your Merlin (M4) and reading Merlin tablature, along with the basic Merlin chords and a selection of easy strumming and picking patterns you can use on their own or as a starting point to create your own accompaniments.

A few words on playing technique:

You can fret with your fingers, a noter, a bottleneck or a lap steel bar to get an especially haunting sound. For right hand picking, there's a lot of possibilities, too: picking with your fingers, fingerpicks or with a plectrum like a "normal" guitar.

Feel free to experiment and see what you like.

Wishing you lots of fun and a happy Merlin Christmas,

Thomas Balinger

Contents

Songs

Appendix

Deck the halls

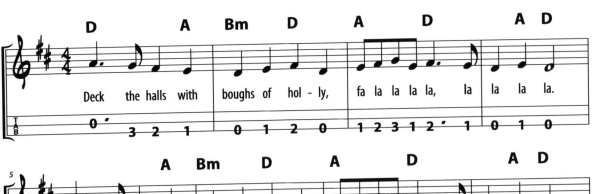

D   A   Bm   D   A   D   A D

Deck the halls with boughs of hol - ly, fa la la la la, la la la la.

A   Bm   D   A   D   A D

'Tis the sea - son to be jol - ly, fa la la la la, la la la la.

A   D   D   Bm   E^7 A

Don we now our gay ap - par - el, fa la la la la la la la la.

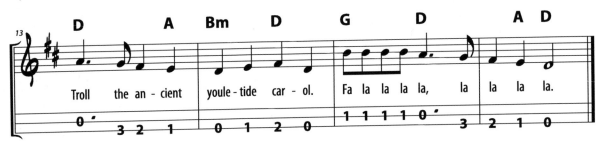

D   A   Bm   D   G   D   A D

Troll the an - cient youle - tide car - ol. Fa la la la la, la la la la.

2. See the blazing Yule before us,
   fa-la-la-la-la, la-la-la-la,
   strike the lamp and join the chorus,
   fa-la-la-la-la, la-la-la-la,
   follow me in merry measure,
   fa-la-la-la-la-la, la-la-la,
   while I tell of yuletide treasure,
   fa-la-la-la-la, la-la-la-la.

3. Fast away the old year passes,
   fa-la-la-la-la, la-la-la-la,
   hail the new year, ye lads and lasses,
   fa-la-la-la-la, la-la-la-la,
   sing we joyous all together,
   fa-la-la-la-la, la-la-la-la,
   heedless of the wind and weather,
   fa-la-la-la-la, la-la-la-la.

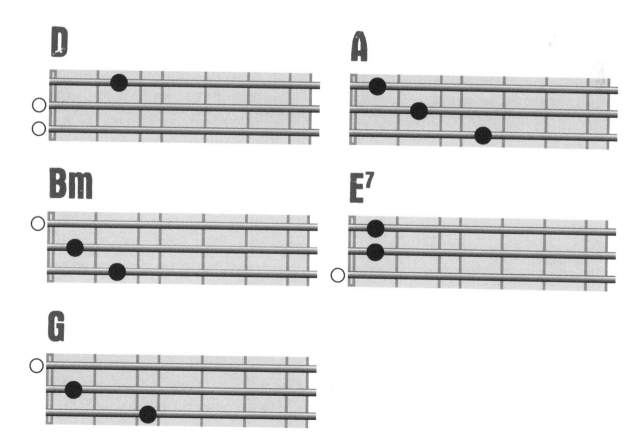

Joy to the world

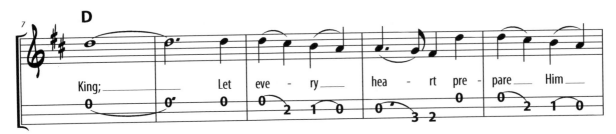

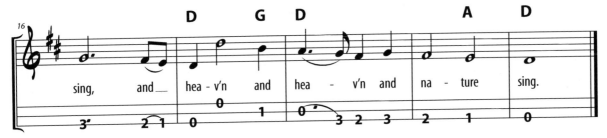

2. Joy to the world, the savior reigns.
   Let men their songs employ.
   While fields and floods, rocks, hills, and plains
   repeat the sounding joy,
   repeat the sounding joy
   repeat, repeat the sounding joy

3. No more let sin and sorrows grow,
   nor thorns infest the ground;
   He comes to make His blessings flow
   far as the curse is found,
   far as the curse is found,
   far as, far as the curse is found.

4. He rules the world with truth and grace,
   And makes the nations prove
   the glories of His righteousness.
   And wonders of His love,
   and wonders of His love,
   and wonders, wonders of His love.

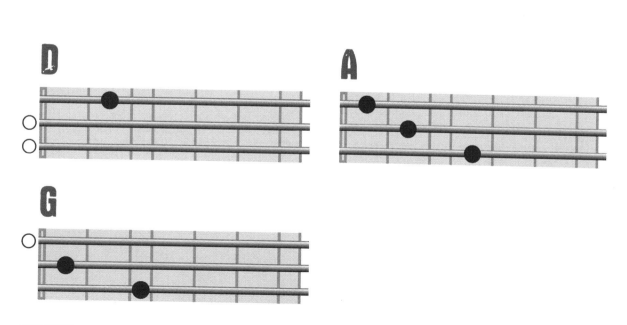

The boar's head carol

The boar's head in hand bear I, be-deck'd with bays and

rose-mar-y; and I pray you, my mas-ters, be mer-ry, quot

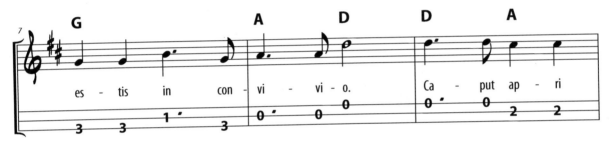

es-tis in con-vi-vi-o. Ca-put ap-ri

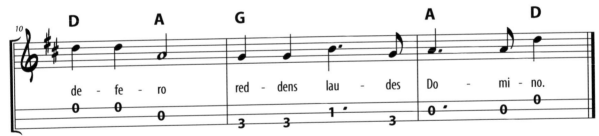

de-fe-ro red-dens lau-des Do - mi-no.

2. The boar's head, as I understand,
   is the rarest dish in all this land,
   which thus bedeck'd with a gay garland,
   let us servire cantico.
   Caput apri defero,
   reddens laudes Domino.

3. Our steward hath provided this
   in honour of the King of Bliss,
   which on this day to be served is,
   in reginensi atrio.
   Caput apri defero,
   reddens laudes Domino.

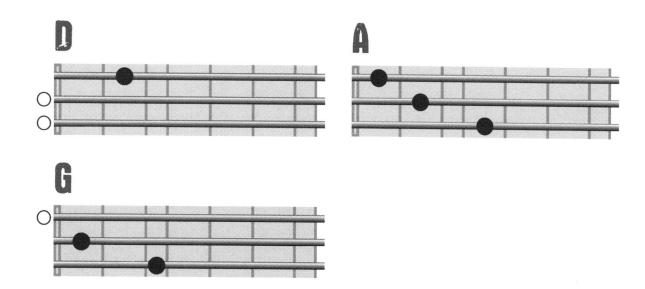

hile shepherds watched

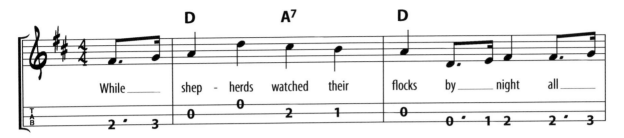

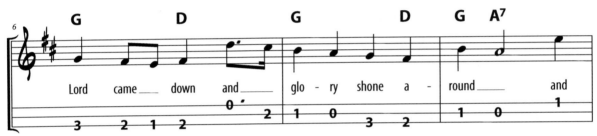

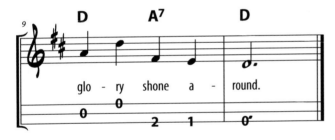

2. "Fear not," he said,
   for mighty dread
   had seized their troubled minds.
   "Glad tidings of great joy I bring
   to you and all mankind,
   to you and all mankind."

3. "To you in David's
   town this day
   is born of David's line.
   The Savior who is Christ the Lord
   and this shall be the sign
   and this shall be the sign."

4. "The heavenly Babe
   you there shall find
   to human view displayed,
   and meanly wrapped in swathing bands,
   and in a manger laid,
   and in a manger laid."

5. Thus spake the seraph,
   and forthwith
   appeared a shining throng
   of angels praising God, who thus
   addressed their joyful song,
   addressed their joyful song.

6. "All glory be to
   God on high
   and to the earth be peace;
   Goodwill henceforth
   from heaven to men
   begin and never cease,
   begin and never cease!"

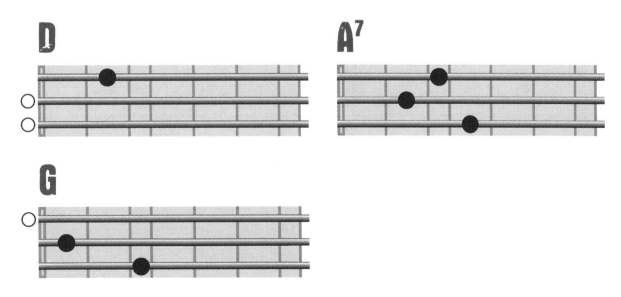

Over the river and through the woods

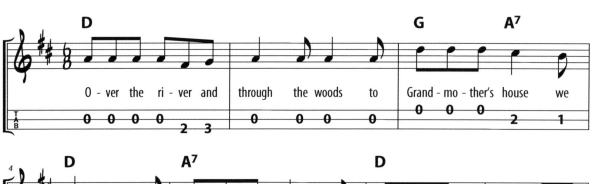

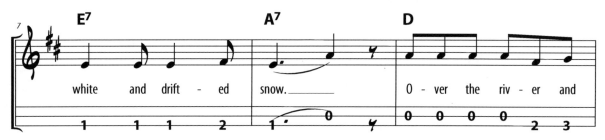

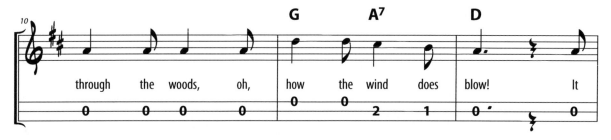

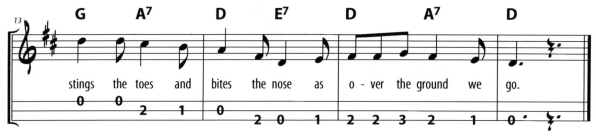

2. Over the river and through the woods,
   to have a first-rate play;
   Oh, hear the bells ring, "Ting-a-ling-ling!"
   Hurrah for Thanksgiving Day!
   Over the river and through the woods,
   trot fast, my dapple gray!
   Spring over the ground, like a hunting hound!
   For this is Thanksgiving Day.

3. Over the river and through the woods,
   and straight through the barnyard gate.
   We seem to go extremely slow
   it is so hard to wait!
   Over the river and through the woods,
   now Grandmother's cap I spy!
   Hurrah for the fun! Is the pudding done?
   Hurrah for the pumpkin pie!

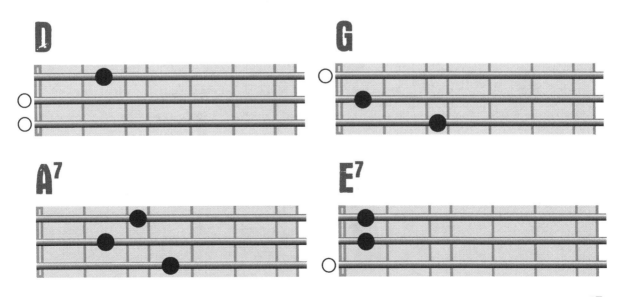

The first Noel

2. They looked up and saw a star
   shining in the east beyond them far,
   and to the earth it gave great light,
   and so it continued both day and night.

3. And by the light of that same star
   three wise men came from country far;
   To seek for a king was their intent,
   and to follow the star wherever it went.

4. This star drew nigh to the northwest,
   o'er Bethlehem it took it rest,
   and there it did both stop and stay
   right over the place where Jesus lay.

5. Then entered in those wise men three
   full reverently upon their knee,
   and offered there in his presence
   their gold, and myrrh, and frankincense.

6. Then let us all with one accord
   sing praises to our heavenly Lord;
   That hath made heaven and earth of naught,
   and with his blood mankind hath bought.

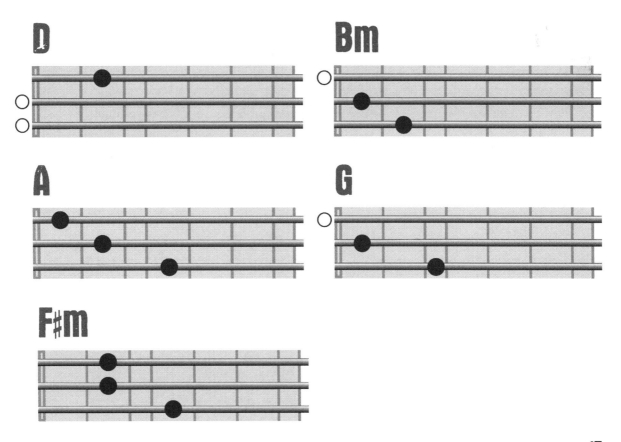

O come, little children

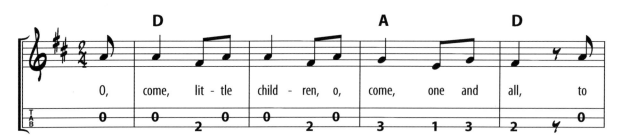

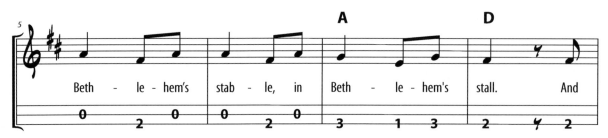

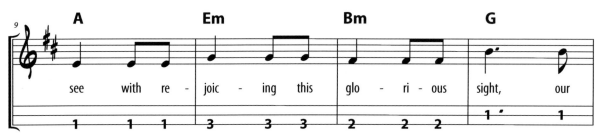

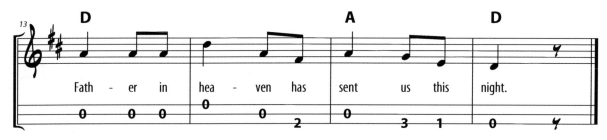

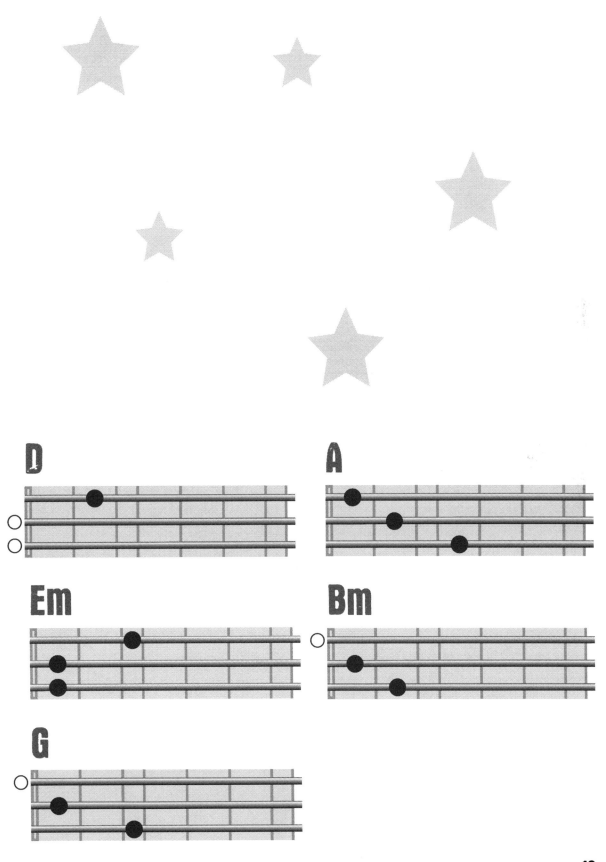

Christ was born on christmas day

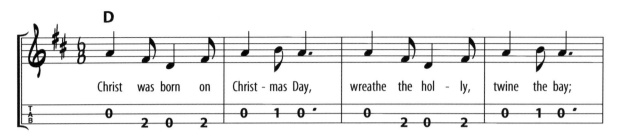

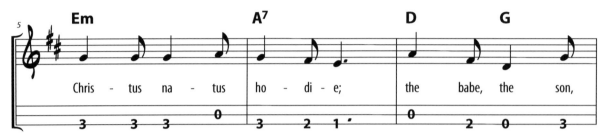

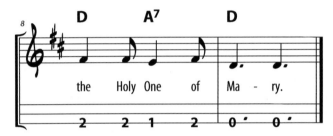

2. He is born to set us free,
   He is born our Lord to be,
   ex Maria Virgine,
   the God, the Lord, by all adored forever.

3. Let the bright red berries glow,
   ev'ry where in goodly show,
   Christus natus hodie;
   the Babe, the Son, the Holy One of Mary.

4. Christian men, rejoice and sing,
   tis the birthday of a King
   ex Maria Virgine;
   The God, the Lord, by all adored forever.

5. Sing out with bliss,
   His name is this: Immanuel!
   As 'twas foretold in days of old,
   by Gabriel.

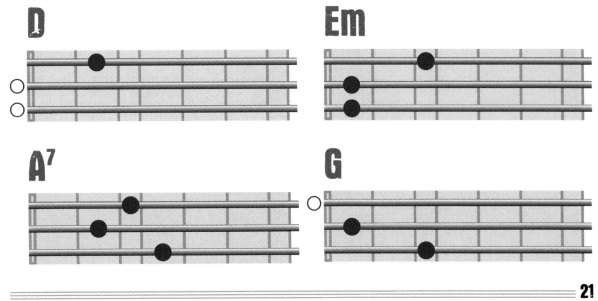

In the bleak midwinter

2. Our God, heaven cannot hold him,
   nor earth sustain;
   Heaven and earth shall flee away
   when he comes to reign;
   In the bleak midwinter
   a stable place sufficed
   the Lord God incarnate,
   Jesus Christ.

3. Enough for him, whom Cherubim
   worship night and day
   a breast full of milk
   and a manger full of hay.
   Enough for him, whom angels
   fall down before,
   the ox and ass and camel
   which adore.

4. Angels and archangels
   may have gathered there,
   Cherubim and seraphim
   thronged the air;
   But his mother only,
   in her maiden bliss,
   worshipped the Beloved
   with a kiss.

5. What can I give him,
   poor as I am?
   If I were a shepherd
   I would bring a lamb,
   if I were a wise man
   I would do my part,
   yet what I can I give Him —
   Give my heart.

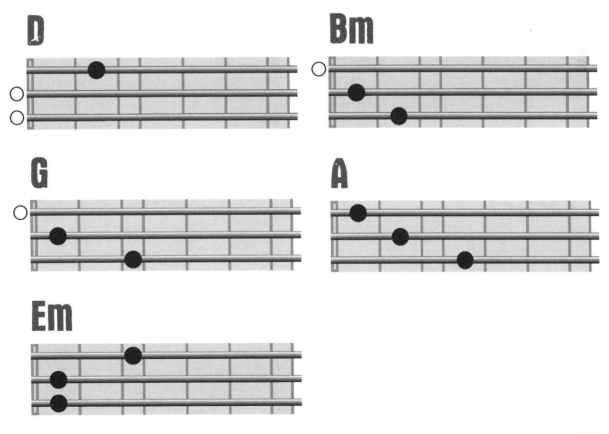

ngels from the realms of glory

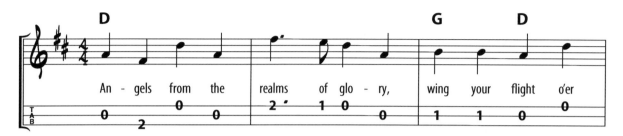

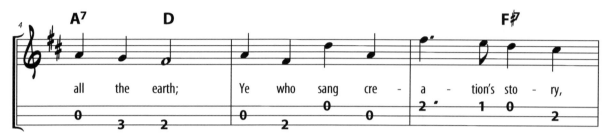

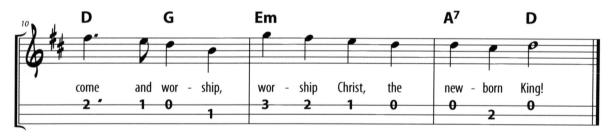

2. Shepherds, in the fields abiding,
   watching o'er your flocks by night,
   God with man is now residing,
   yonder shines the infant Light;
   Come and worship,
   come and worship,
   worship Christ, the newborn King!

3. Sages, leave your contemplations,
   brighter visions beam afar;
   Seek the great desire of nations,
   ye have seen His natal star;
   Come and worship,
   come and worship,
   worship Christ, the newborn King!

4. Saints before the altar bending,
   watching long in hope and fear,
   suddenly the Lord, descending,
   in His temple shall appear:
   Come and worship,
   come and worship,
   worship Christ, the newborn King!

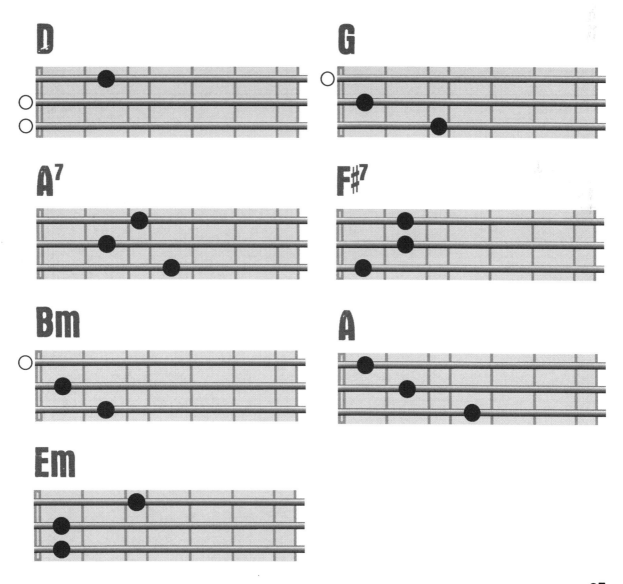

ing Dong! Merrily on high

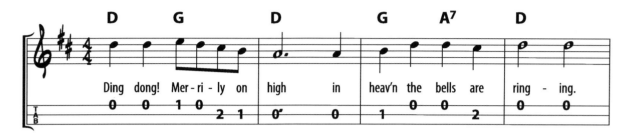

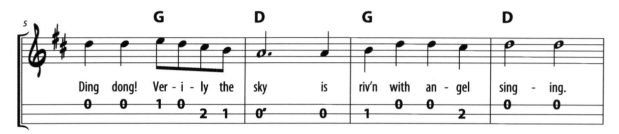

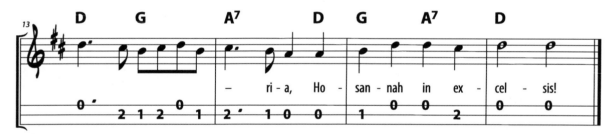

2. E'en so here below, below,
   let steeple bells be swungen,
   and "Io, io, io!"
   by priest and people sungen.

3. Pray you, dutifully prime
   your matin chime, ye ringers;
   May you beautifully rime
   your evetime song, ye singers.

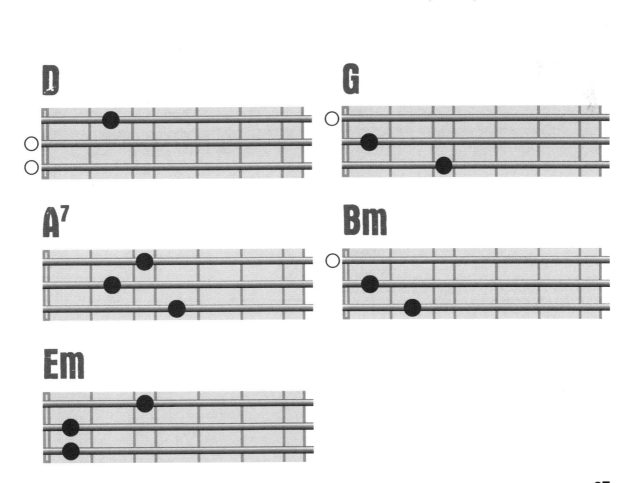

Once in royal David's city

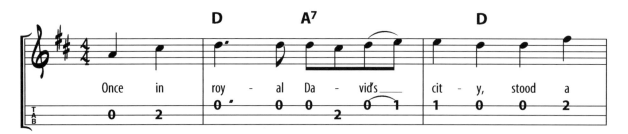

Once in roy - al Da - vid's___ cit - y, stood a

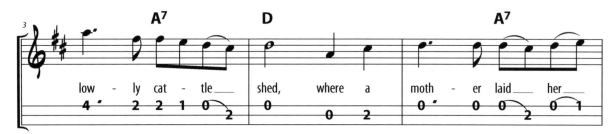

low - ly cat - tle___ shed, where a moth - er laid___ her___

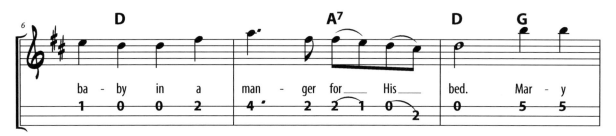

ba - by in a man - ger for___ His___ bed. Mar - y

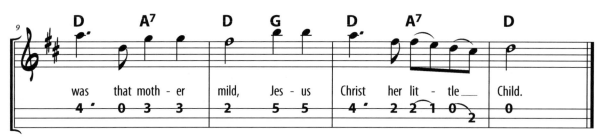

was that moth - er mild, Jes - us Christ her lit - tle___ Child.

2. He came down to earth from heaven,
   who is God and Lord of all,
   and His shelter was a stable,
   and His cradle was a stall:
   With the poor, and mean, and lowly,
   lived on earth our Saviour holy.

3. For He is our childhood's pattern;
   Day by day, like us, He grew;
   He was little, weak, and helpless,
   tears and smiles, like us He knew;
   And He cares when we are sad,
   and he shares when we are glad.

4. And our eyes at last shall see Him,
   through His own redeeming love;
   For that Child so dear and gentle,
   is our Lord in heaven above:
   And He leads His children on,
   to the place where He is gone.

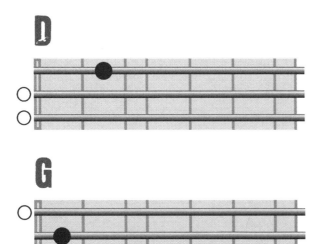

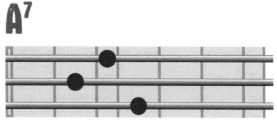

ngels we have heard on high

An - gels we have | heard on high | sweet - ly sing - ing | o'er the plains.

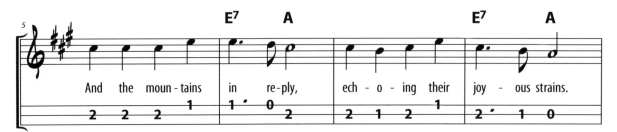

And the moun - tains | in re - ply, | ech - o - ing their | joy - ous strains.

Glo - - - - - - - ri - a

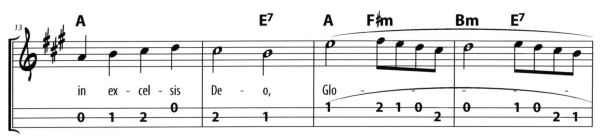

in ex - cel - sis De - o, | Glo - - - - -

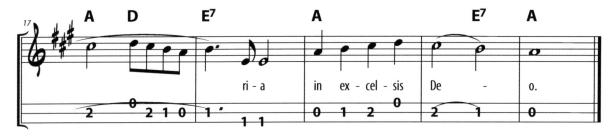

ri - a | in ex - cel - sis De - - o.

2. Shepherds, why this Jubilee?
   Why your joyous strains prolong?
   What the gladsome tidings be
   which inspire your heavenly song?

3. Come to Bethlehem and see
   Him whose birth the angels sing;
   Come, adore on bended knee
   Christ, the Lord, the newborn King

4. See Him in a manger laid
   Jesus, Lord of heaven and earth!
   Mary, Joseph, lend your aid,
   with us sing our Savior's birth.

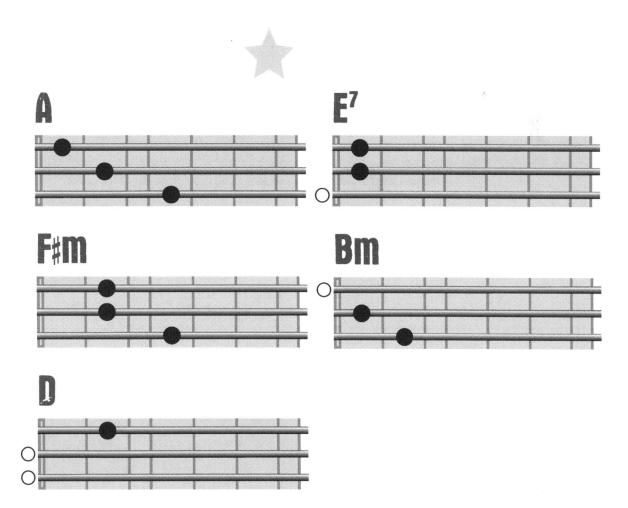

way in a manger

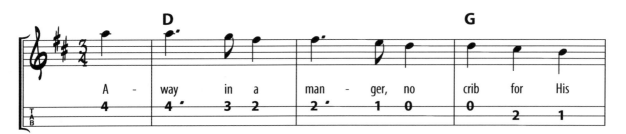

A - way in a man - ger, no crib for His

bed, the litt - le Lord Je - sus laid down His sweet

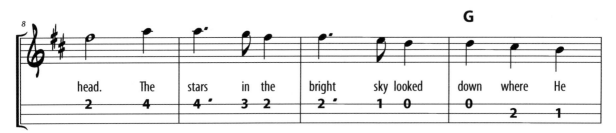

head. The stars in the bright sky looked down where He

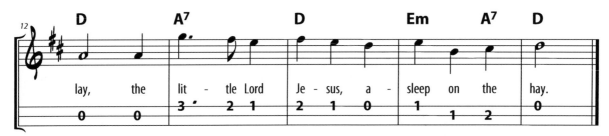

lay, the lit - tle Lord Je - sus, a - sleep on the hay.

2. The cattle are lowing
   the poor baby wakes.
   But little Lord Jesus
   no crying He makes.
   I love Thee, Lord Jesus,
   look down from the sky
   and stay by my side,
   'til morning is nigh.

3. Be near me, Lord Jesus,
   I ask Thee to stay.
   Close by me forever
   and love me I pray.
   Bless all the dear children
   in Thy tender care
   and take us to heaven
   to live with Thee there.

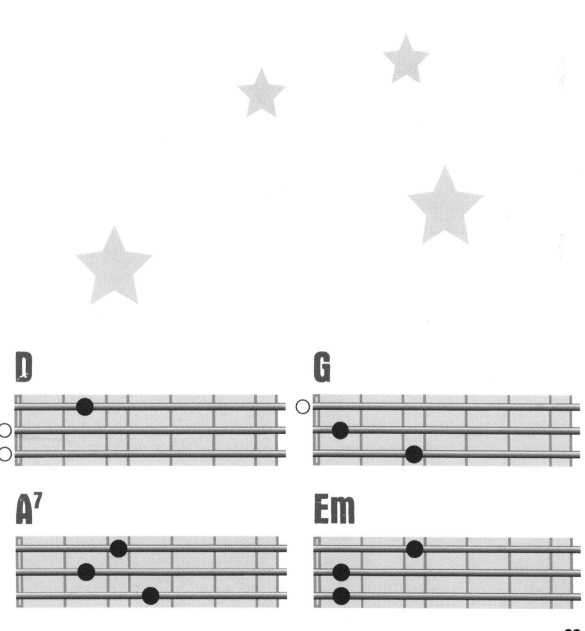

Go, tell it on the mountain

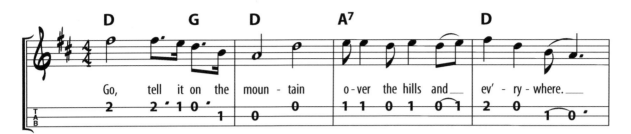

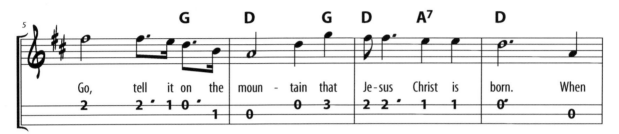

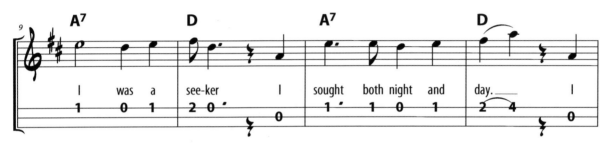

2. He made me a watchman upon the city wall,
   and if I am a Christian I am the least of all.

3. 'T was a lowly manger that Jesus Christ was born.
   The Lord sent down an angel that bright and glorious morn'.

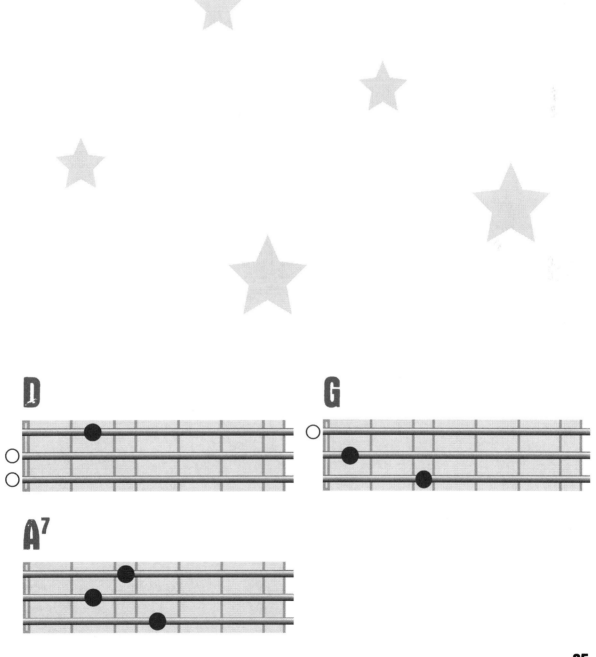

Jingle Bells

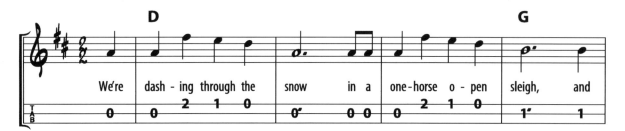

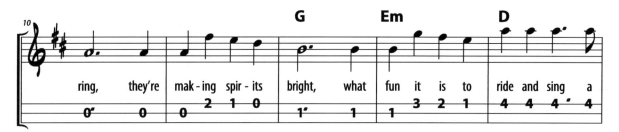

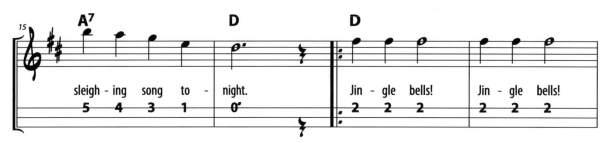

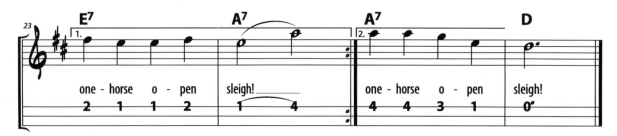

2. A day or two ago I thought I'd take a ride,
   and soon Miss Fannie Bright was seated by my side.
   The horse was lean and lank, misfortune seemed his lot,
   he got into a drifted bank and we got upsot.

3. A day or two ago, the story I must tell.
   I went out on the snow, and on my back I fell;
   A gent was riding by in a one-horse open sleigh,
   he laughed as there I sprawling lie, But quickly drove away.

4. Now the ground is white, go it while you're young,
   take the girls tonight and sing this sleighing song.
   Just get a bobtailed bay, two-forty for his speed,
   then hitch him to an open sleigh, and crack! You'll take the lead.

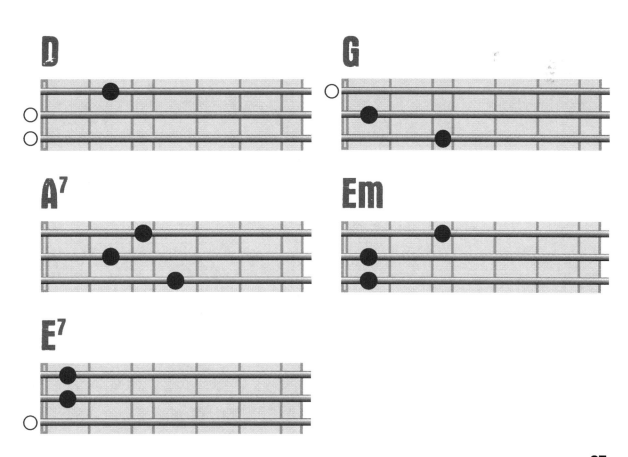

e wish you a merry Christmas

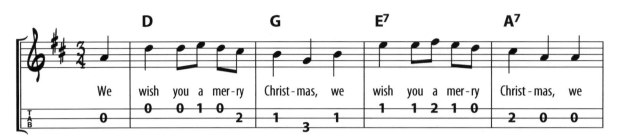

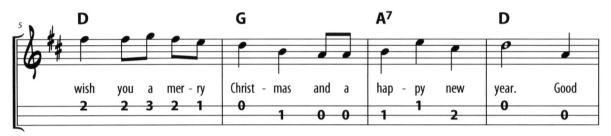

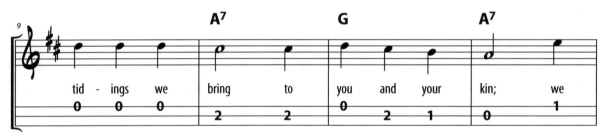

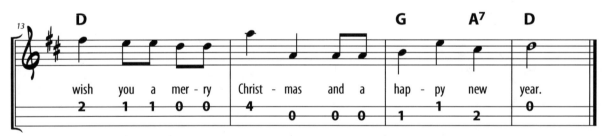

2. Now bring us some figgy pudding (3x),
   and bring some out here!

3. For we all like figgy pudding,
   we all like figgy pudding (2x),
   so bring some out here!

4. And we won't go until we've got some,
   we won't go until we've got some (2x),
   so bring some out here!

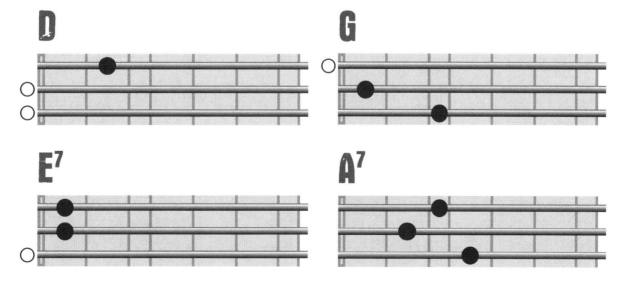

saw three ships

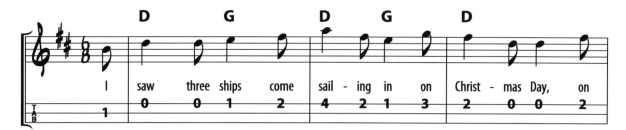

2. And what was in those ships all three,
   on Christmas Day, on Christmas Day?
   And what was in those ships all three,
   on Christmas Day in the morning?

3. The Virgin Mary and Christ were there,
   on Christmas Day, on Christmas Day;
   The Virgin Mary and Christ were there,
   on Christmas Day in the morning.

4. Pray, wither sailed those ships all three,
   on Christmas Day, on Christmas Day;
   Pray, wither sailed those ships all three,
   on Christmas Day in the morning?

5. O they sailed into Bethlehem,
   on Christmas Day, on Christmas Day;
   O they sailed into Bethlehem,
   on Christmas Day in the morning.

6. And all the bells on earth shall ring,
   on Christmas Day, on Christmas Day;
   And all the bells on earth shall ring,
   on Christmas Day in the morning.

7. And all the Angels in Heaven shall sing,
   on Christmas Day, on Christmas Day;
   And all the Angels in Heaven shall sing,
   on Christmas Day in the morning.

8. And all the souls on earth shall sing,
   on Christmas Day, on Christmas Day;
   And all the souls on earth shall sing,
   on Christmas Day in the morning.

9. Then let us all rejoice again,
   on Christmas Day, on Christmas Day;
   Then let us all rejoice again,
   on Christmas Day in the morning.

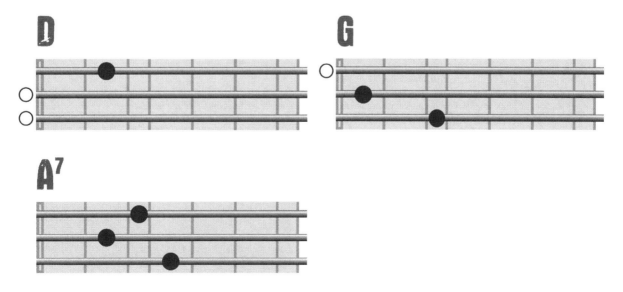

Still, still, still

Still, still, still, the night is cold and chill! The

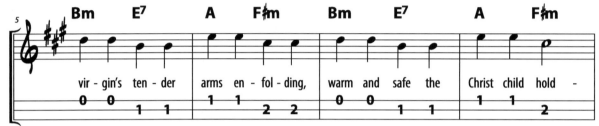

vir - gin's ten - der arms en - fol - ding, warm and safe the Christ child hold -

ing. Still, still, still, the night is cold and chill.

2. Dream, dream, dream.
   He sleeps, the Savior King.
   While guardian angels watch beside Him,
   Mary tenderly will guide Him.
   Dream, dream, dream.
   He sleeps, the Savior King.

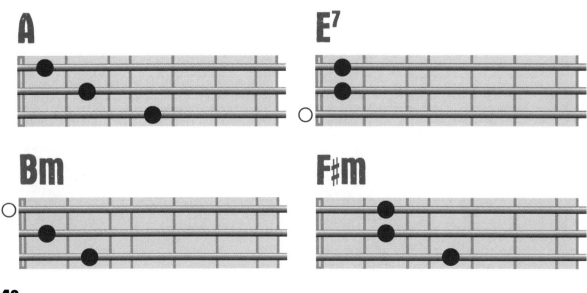

Up on the housetop

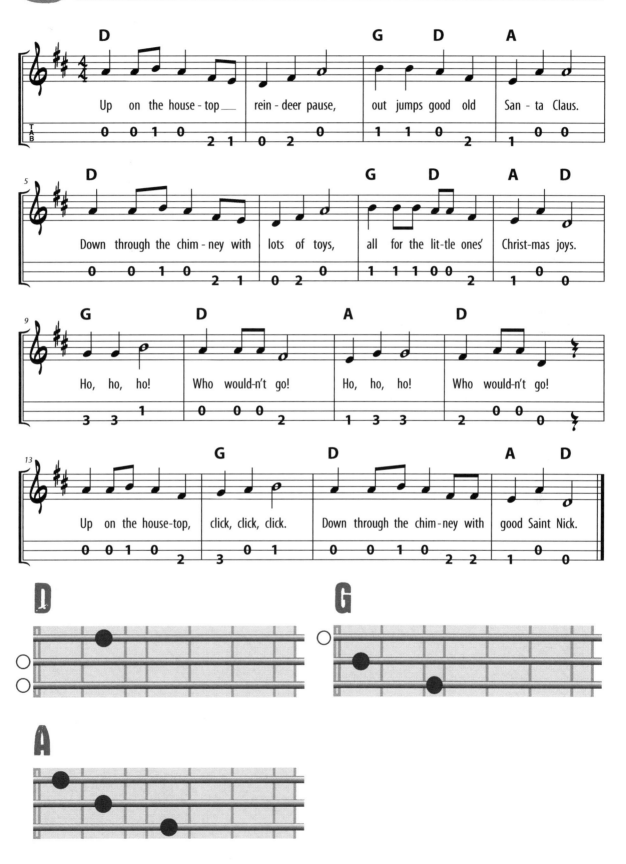

O Sanctissima

O thou hap - py, O thou ho - ly,

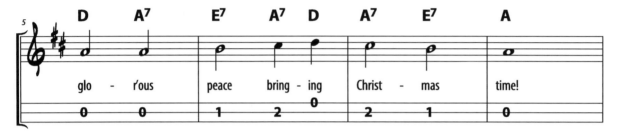

glo - r'ous peace bring - ing Christ - mas time!

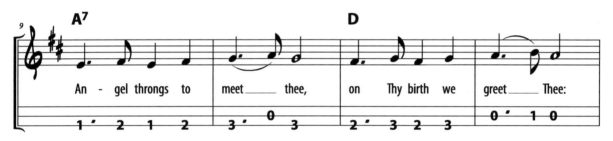

An - gel throngs to meet thee, on Thy birth we greet Thee:

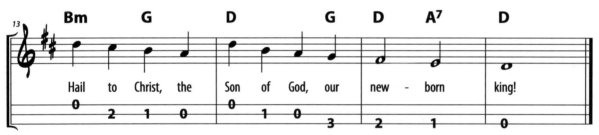

Hail to Christ, the Son of God, our new - born king!

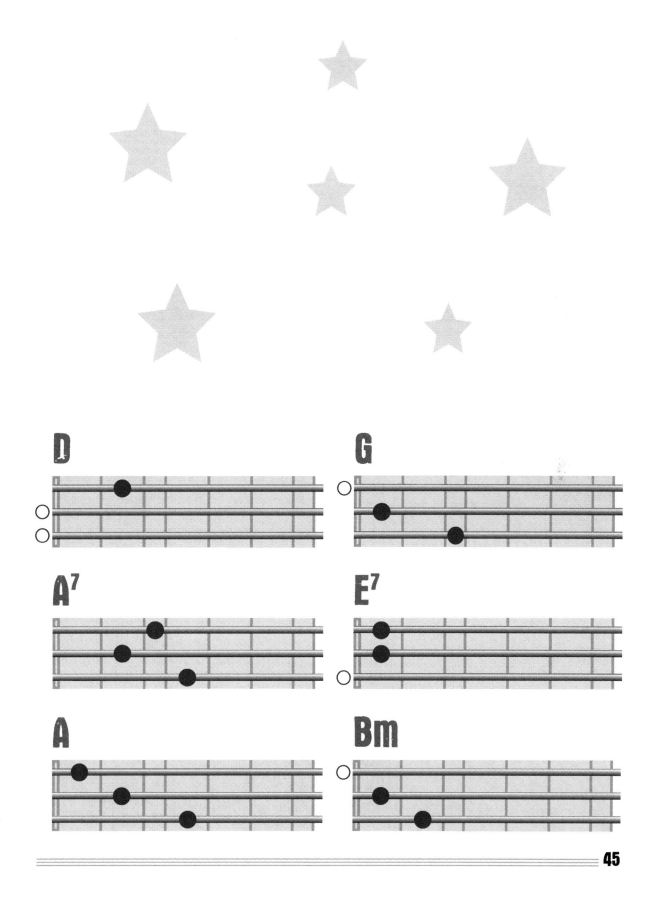

ilent night

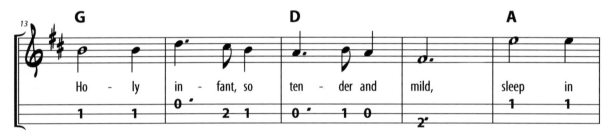

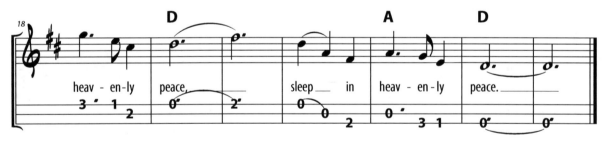

2. Silent night, Holy night!
   Son of God, love's pure light.
   Radiant beams from thy holy face.
   With the dawn of redeeming grace,
   Jesus, Lord at thy birth,
   Jesus, Lord at thy birth.

3. Silent night, Holy night!
   Shepherds quake at the sight.
   Glories stream from heaven above.
   Heavenly, hosts sing Hallelujah,
   Christ the Savior is born,
   Christ the Savior is born.

D

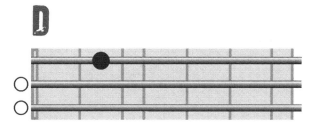

A

G

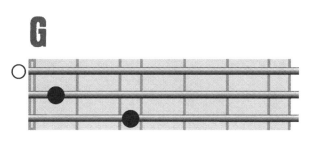

Twinkle, twinkle little star

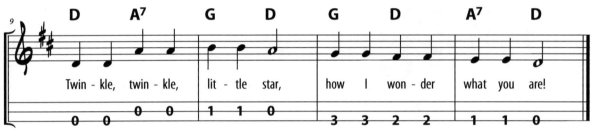

2. When the blazing sun is gone,
   when he nothing shines upon,
   then you show your little light,
   twinkle, twinkle, all the night.

3. Then the traveller in the dark,
   thanks you for your tiny spark,
   he could not see which way to go,
   if you did not twinkle so.

4. In the dark blue sky you keep,
   and often through my curtains peep,
   for you never shut your eye,
   till the sun is in the sky.

5. As your bright and tiny spark,
   lights the traveller in the dark,
   though I know not what you are,
   twinkle, twinkle, little star.

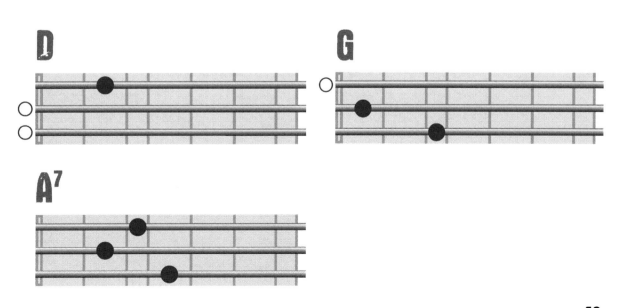

Hark! The herald angels sing

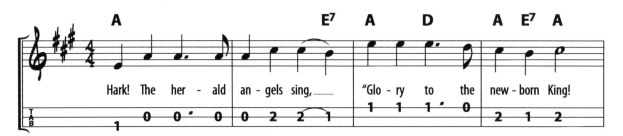

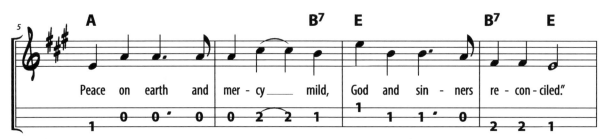

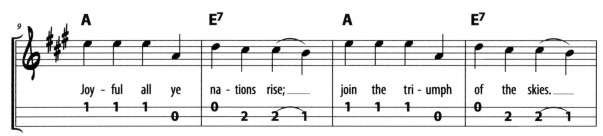

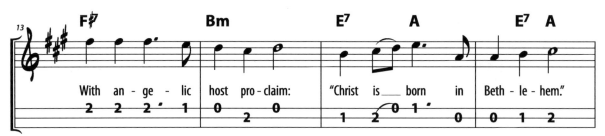

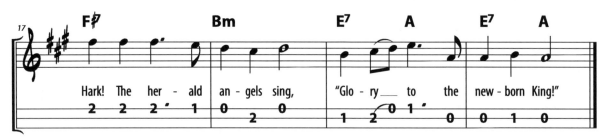

2. Christ by highest heav'n adored,
   Christ the everlasting Lord!
   Late in time behold Him come,
   offspring of a virgin's womb.
   Veiled in flesh the Godhead see,
   hail the incarnate deity!
   Pleased as man with man to dwell,
   Jesus, our Emmanuel,
   Hark! The herald angels sing,
   "Glory to the newborn king!"

3. Hail the heav'n-born prince of peace,
   hail the son of righteousness!
   Light and life to all He brings,
   Ris'n with healing in His wings.
   Mild He lays His glory by,
   born that man no more may die!
   Born to raise the sons of earth,
   born to give them second birth!
   Hark! The herald angels sing,
   "Glory to the newborn king!"

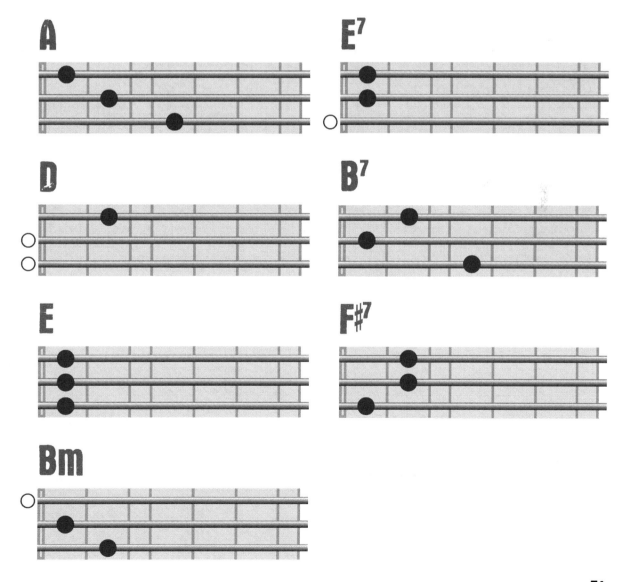

It came upon a midnight clear

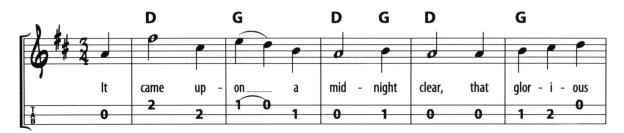

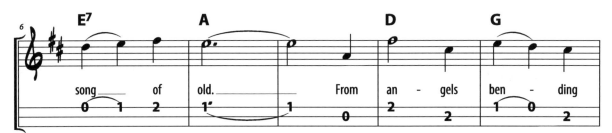

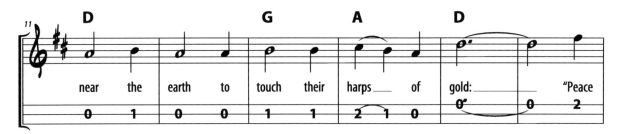

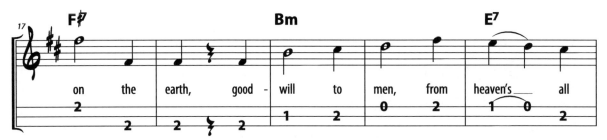

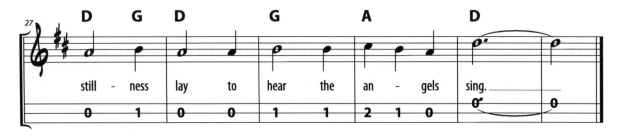

2. Still through the cloven skies they come,
   with peaceful wings unfurled;
   And still their heavenly music floats
   o'er all the weary world:
   Above its sad and lowly plains
   they bend on hovering wing,
   and ever o'er its Babel sounds
   the blessed angels sing.

3. O ye beneath life's crushing load,
   whose forms are bending low,
   who toil along the climbing way
   with painful steps and slow;
   Look now, for glad and golden hours
   come swiftly on the wing;
   Oh rest beside the weary road
   and hear the angels sing.

4. For lo! the days are hastening on,
   by prophets seen of old,
   when with the ever-circling years
   shall come the time foretold,
   when the new heaven and earth shall own
   the Prince of Peace, their King,
   and the whole world send back the song
   which now the angels sing.

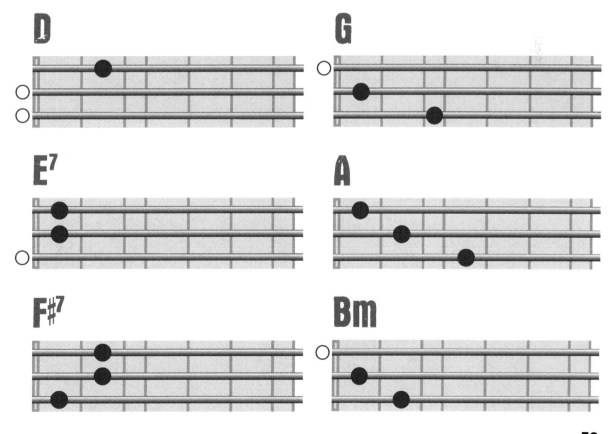

He is born, the holy child

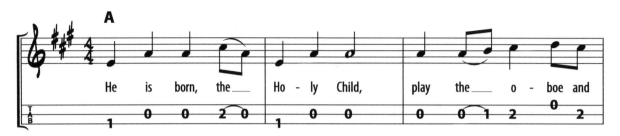

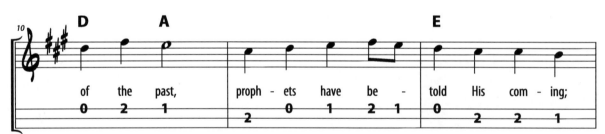

Chorus
He is born, the holy child,
play the oboe and bagpipes merrily!
He is born, the holy child,
sing we all of the Savior mild.

2. O how lovely, O how pure,
   is this perfect child of heaven;
   O how lovely, O how pure,
   gracious gift of God to man!
   He is born, the holy child . . .

3. Jesus, Lord of all the world,
   coming as a child among us,
   Jesus, Lord of all the world,
   grant to us Thy heavenly peace.
   He is born, the holy child . . .

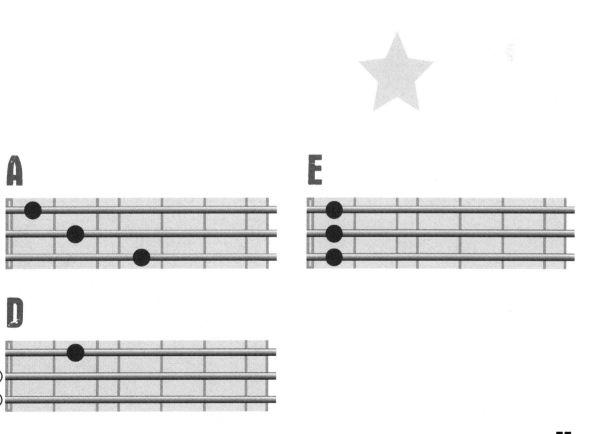

Tuning your Merlin

In this book I use standard D tuning.

In this tuning the strings of your Merlin are tuned to:

-   D (melody string, double string) - both strings are tuned to D.
-   A (middle string)
-   D (bass string)

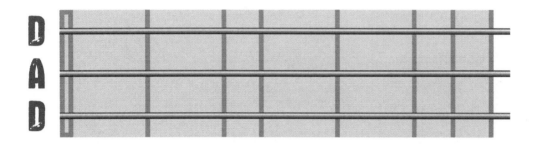

Tuning your Merlin is easiest using an electronic tuner.
Nevertheless, it's a good idea to practice tuning by ear, too.
So here's how to properly tune your Merlin by ear:

1. First, using a reference tone from a guitar or piano, tune the bass string to the note D.

2. Then press the bass string down at the 4th fret and tune the middle A string to this note.

3. Now press the middle A string down at the 3rd fret and tune the melody string(s) to this note (D).

Check your tuning:
Play all strings. This should result in a nice and full sounding D major chord – the easiest chord on the Merlin (strictly said this is a D major chord with the third missing).
If this chord does sound "dirty" or not like a chord at all, check points 1–3 again.

Merlin tablature

I've notated the songs' melodies in standard notation and tablature. If you don't want to read music, simply use the tablature. Here's how it's read:

- Horizontal lines represent the strings, vertical lines the frets of your Merlin.
- Numbers indicate the frets.
- Open strings are indicated by an "0".

So the passage below (the first bar of "Jingle Bells") reads:

- first play the A string twice (open string),
- followed by the D string, 2nd fret,
- the D string, 1st fret,
- the D string (open string),
- and the A string (open string).

The notes on the Merlin fretboard:

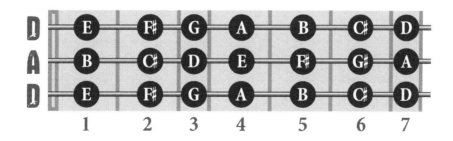

Basic chords

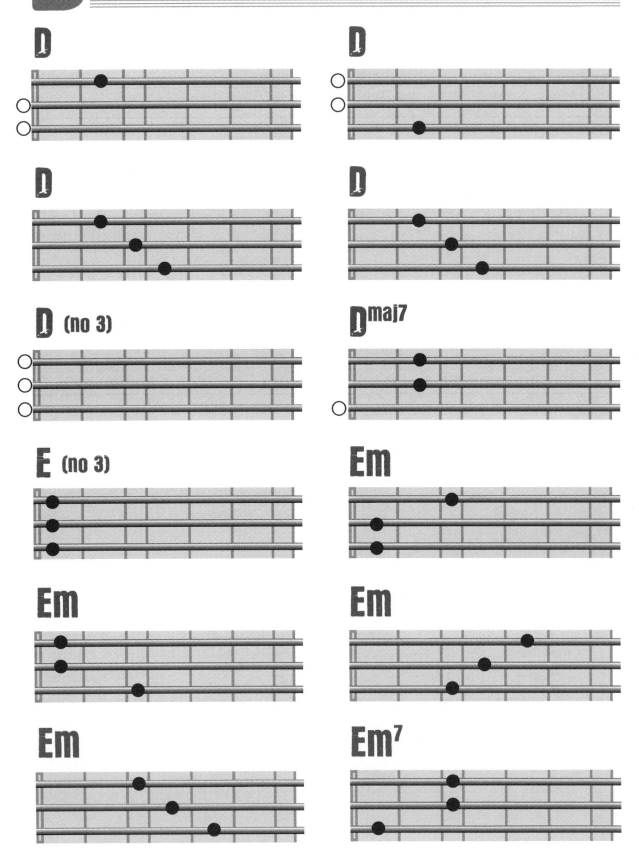

D

D

D

D

D (no 3)

D maj7

E (no 3)

Em

Em

Em

Em

Em 7

Basic chords

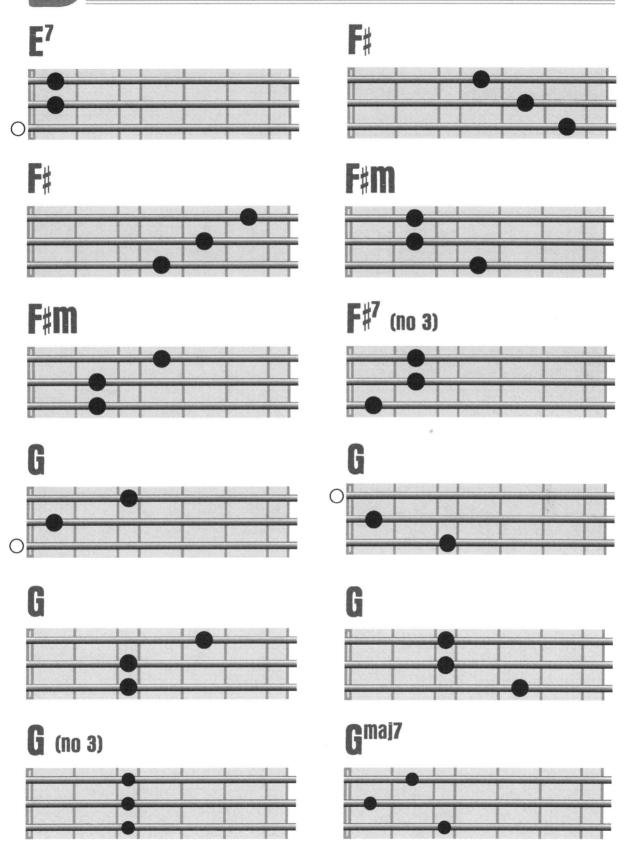asic chords

Basic chords

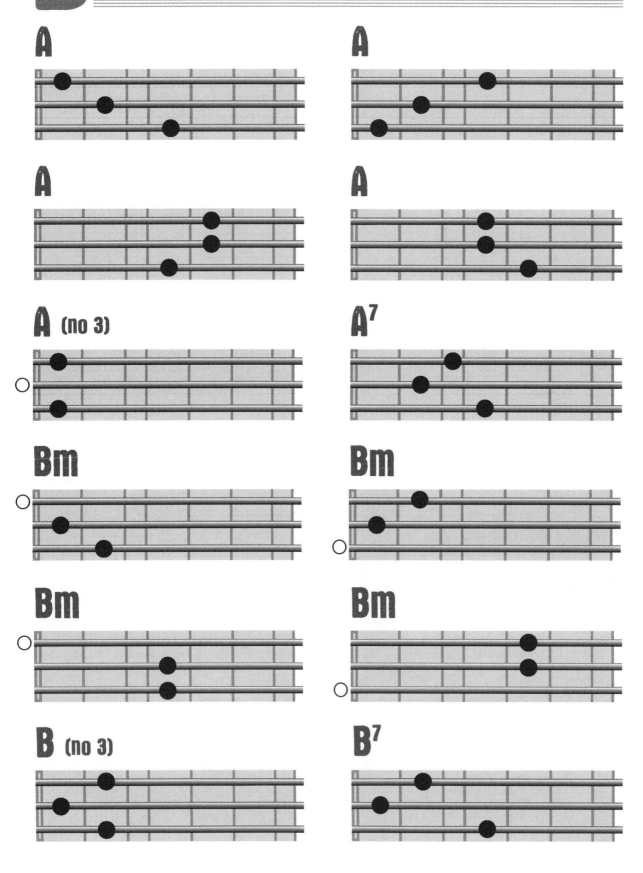

Strumming patterns

The following is a selection of basic strumming patterns which you can use for song accompaniment. These are just for starters – you'll soon use other, more elaborate patterns or invent your own. Feel free to use a pick or your finger(s) for strumming - basically whatever feels best.

Here's how they're read:

- The horizontal lines represent the strings of your Merlin.
  Downstroke (strumming in the direction of the floor): arrow upward
  Upstroke: arrow downward.
- The length of the arrows indicates which strings to strum.
- Each of these pattern shows a whole measure.

For song accompaniment you can choose (and also combine) whatever pattern feels best to you, but keep in mind to match the pattern's time to the time of the song, e.g. for a song in 4/4 time only use strumming patterns in 4/4 time.
Songs in 2/2 time can be played using strumming patterns in 4/4 time.

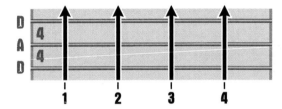
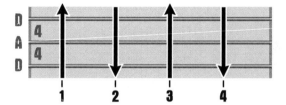

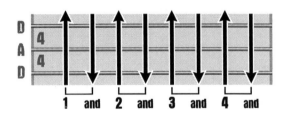
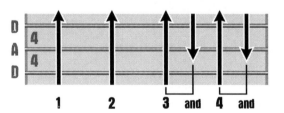

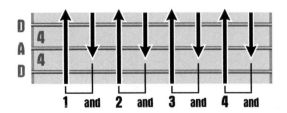
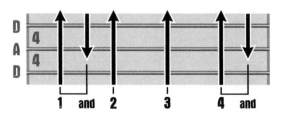

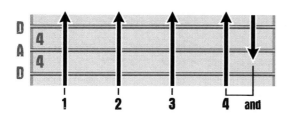

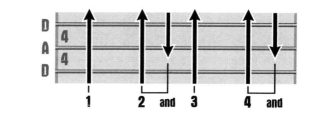

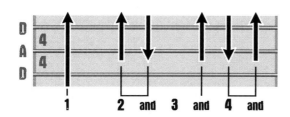

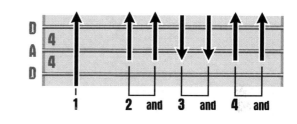

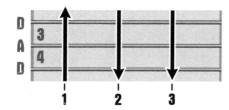

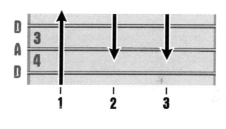

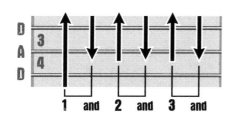

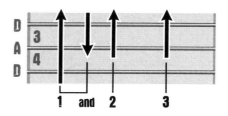

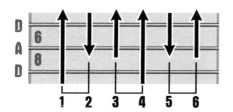

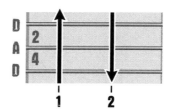

Picking patterns

Many songs sound particularly good when played using a picking pattern. The basic ideas is this: instead of picking all the notes of a chord simultaneously with your finger(s) or a pick, you play them successively, one after the other. Picking patterns are commonly used for longer musical sections (or even whole songs) and adapted to the chord changes if necessary.

As in tablature, horizontal lines represent the strings of your Merlin. The time signature is notated at the beginning of the pattern as a fraction (e.g. 4/4 for songs in 4/4 time).
The letters T, I and M indicate the fingers of the picking hand.
There are a few things to keep in mind when using picking patterns:
Obviously, the pattern's time signature has to match that of the song. In some cases, the pattern may have to be adapted to a certain chord or a chord change, but most of the time you can use the following simple rule:

* pick the D (melody) string with middle finger
* pick the A string with your index finger
* pick the D string (bass string) with your thumb

One of the best ways to practise picking patterns is to play them on open strings until the movement of your fingers becomes second nature – practicing this way ensures you'll be able to concentrate on more important things when it's time to play the song. When the picking pattern has been "automized" to a certain degree it's time to add chords and chord changes. Take your time because nothing sounds worse than a "stuttering" picking pattern interfering with a smooth chord change.
On the next page you'll find some basic picking patterns. These are of course just a small selection from the multitude of possible patterns, meant to whet your appetite – you'll soon find varying patterns and inventing new ones can be lots of fun!

For a start, you may want to try:
* Combining different picking patterns
  (e. g. one for the verse and one for the chorus).
* Combining picking patterns with strumming patterns.
* Mixing picking patterns with melody lines and damping techniques.

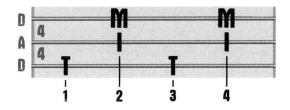

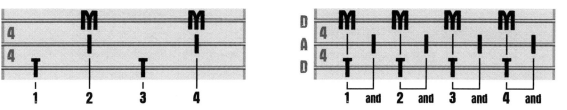

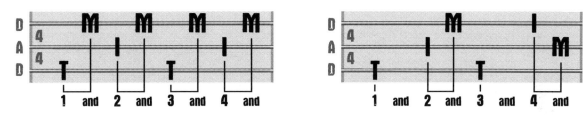

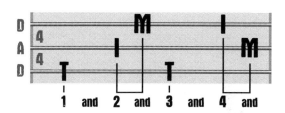

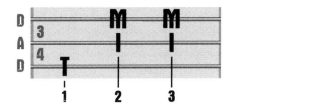

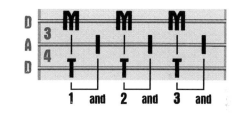

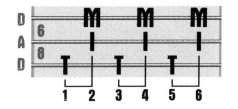

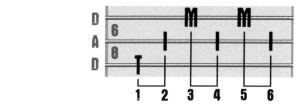

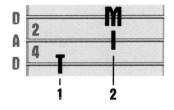

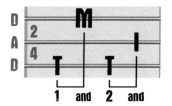

Made in the USA
Las Vegas, NV
16 November 2020

10971240R00037